IT'S TIME TO EAT GERMAN CHOCOLATE CAKE

It's Time to Eat GERMAN CHOCOLATE CAKE

Walter the Educator

Silent King Books
A WhichHead Entertainment Imprint

Copyright © 2025 by Walter the Educator

All rights reserved. No part of this book may be reproduced in any manner whatsoever without written per- mission except in the case of brief quotations embodied in critical articles and reviews.

First Printing, 2024

Disclaimer

This book is a literary work; the story is not about specific persons, locations, situations, and/or circumstances unless mentioned in a historical context. Any resemblance to real persons, locations, situations, and/or circumstances is coincidental. This book is for entertainment and informational purposes only. The author and publisher offer this information without warranties expressed or implied. No matter the grounds, neither the author nor the publisher will be accountable for any losses, injuries, or other damages caused by the reader's use of this book. The use of this book acknowledges an understanding and acceptance of this disclaimer.

It's Time to Eat GERMAN CHOCOLATE CAKE is a collectible early learning book by Walter the Educator suitable for all ages belonging to Walter the Educator's Time to Eat Book Series. Collect more books at WaltertheEducator.com

USE THE EXTRA SPACE TO TAKE NOTES AND DOCUMENT YOUR MEMORIES

GERMAN CHOCOLATE CAKE

It's time to eat, hip hip hooray,

It's Time to Eat
German Chocolate Cake

German Chocolate Cake today!

So sweet and soft, with frosting high,

A chocolate tower to the sky!

Coconut and nuts on top,

With each bite, we just can't stop!

Chocolate layers rich and bold,

Yummy stories to be told.

We grab our forks and take a bite,

Our eyes grow big with pure delight!

Sweet and chewy, soft and grand,

German Chocolate tastes so planned.

Mom cuts slices, nice and neat,

Puts them on our plates so sweet.

Every forkful tastes so fine,

Chocolate cake, it's party time!

It's Time to Eat German Chocolate Cake

Drizzle here and drizzle there,

Chocolate frosting everywhere!

Lick our fingers, take a taste,

Not one crumb will go to waste!

It's sticky, gooey, full of fun,

German Cake for everyone!

Coconut makes a happy crunch,

This cake could be our lunch!

With every bite, we laugh and cheer,

The best dessert is finally here!

German Chocolate makes us smile,

We'll sit and eat a while.

One more bite and then some more,

We love this cake, that's for sure!

Every taste is pure delight,

It's Time to Eat
German Chocolate Cake

A chocolate dream so bright.

Plates are empty, tummies full,

German Cake, so wonderful!

We clap our hands and dance around,

For the best cake we have found.

Now it's time to say goodnight,

But cake dreams sparkle bright.

German Chocolate, sweet and true,

It's Time to Eat German Chocolate Cake

We'll eat you soon, hooray for you!

ABOUT THE CREATOR

Walter the Educator is one of the pseudonyms for Walter Anderson. Formally educated in Chemistry, Business, and Education, he is an educator, an author, a diverse entrepreneur, and he is the son of a disabled war veteran.
"Walter the Educator" shares his time between educating and creating. He holds interests and owns several creative projects that entertain, enlighten, enhance, and educate, hoping to inspire and motivate you. Follow, find new works, and stay up to date with Walter the Educator™

at WaltertheEducator.com

www.ingramcontent.com/pod-product-compliance
Lightning Source LLC
LaVergne TN
LVHW012052070526
838201LV00082B/3989